The Little Book of 101 Grandad Jokes

This book is dedicated to my own grandchildren Eden, Harry, Liv, Georgie and Arlen.

You can download the free audio book read by the author at:

phil-lancaster.com/101-jokes-audio.

Contents

1. Titanic

Grandad tried to warn everyone that the Titanic was going to hit an iceberg and sink. But no one would listen. He was screaming and shouting but they all told him to be quiet. They weren't interested in what he had to say. But he just got louder and louder.

In the end, they had to eject him from the movie theatre.

2. Ballet

I was pleased that my grandad was able to come to my ballet concert. After it was over, he said to me "I noticed that you all spent a lot of time on your tippy toes."

"That's right, Grandad," I replied.

"Why don't they just get taller girls?" he asked.

3. Lifesavers

Grandad asked me the other day if I knew who had invented lifesavers. When I told him I didn't, he said "I don't know either, but I heard he made a mint."

4. Milk

My grandad and I were in the supermarket to get milk. When the cashier asked him if he wanted it in a plastic bag, he said "No, just leave it in the carton." I was so embarrassed.

But not as much as when another checkout chick asked him if he wanted paper or plastic for his groceries.

"Either," he said, "I'm bisacktual."

I didn't even know he knew stuff like that.

5. Cemetery

When we drove past the cemetery, Grandad said "You know that's the dead centre of town." While we were all groaning, he added "But you mustn't bury me there." When we asked why not, he said "Because I'm not dead yet."

6. Jobs

Grandad was reminiscing again. "When I was a kid," he said, "my first job was in a bakery." I waited. "I kneaded the dough, you see, and I had to make a crust somehow. But I got fired in the end. They said I loafed around too much.

"After that, I got a job in a factory that recycled soft drink cans by crushing them. It was soda pressing.

"I decided to give the recycling industry one more go and went to work in a shoe recycling plant. But to be honest, it was sole destroying.

"But the next job was much better. I was working at a toy factory and warehouse. There were just two of us on the production line for Dracula figures, so I had to make every second Count.

"Then I got a job as a librarian. But I had a lot of trouble separating fact from fiction.

"I do look fondly back on my time at the calendar factory. Unfortunately, they let me go after I took a couple of days off."

My eyes were sore from being rolled so much.

7. Scuba Divers

Grandad and I (I used to say me and Grandad, but he told me that's wrong and he seems to know stuff like that) were watching a marine program on TV and I asked him why the scuba divers fell backwards into the water. He said it was because if they fell forwards, they'd still be in the boat.

8. Haircut

I could see that Grandad had been to the barber so I foolishly said "Did you get a haircut, Grandad?" And of course, he replied "No, I got them all cut." So predictable, but funny too. I groaned, though.

9. Spider

Grandad was telling me that he found a big spider in the kitchen last night. I had a little shiver. He said he was going to kill it, but Grandma told him to take it out instead.

I swear I didn't see this coming.

"So I took him out to dinner and a show. He turned out to be a real cool guy. Wants to be a web designer."

10. Cage Fight

Sometimes I don't know what to make of Grandad. Though he's in his seventies, he does long bike rides, lifts weights and years ago got a black belt in Goju-Kai karate. So when he told us he'd taken up cage fighting, it was at least possible. But then he said "I had my first cage fight last night. That budgie didn't know what hit him."

Later on, Grandad told us "I had another fighting joke for you.

"But I forgot the punch line."

11. Pre-School

Grandad often tells us stories about our Mum when she was little, but I'm pretty sure this one isn't true. "You know," he said, "when your mother was in pre-school, all the kids had to have a nap after lunch. But the police had to be called in to have a word with your Mum. She was resisting a rest."

"Next," he said "there was a kidnapping at the pre-school.

"But he woke up, so there was no problem."

12. Blind Deer

"What do you call a deer with no eyes?" said Grandad. "Dunno," said me.

"No idea (no-eyed deer)" said Grandad.

"What do you call a dead deer with no eyes?" said Grandad. I just rolled my eyes.

"Still no idea," said Grandad.

Thought it was a bit sick, myself.

13. Sick

Funny thing, what I think of as "sick" jokes, Grandad says aren't. He says they're just corny. Or rude. He says the original sick joke had a very specific question and answer format. He also said that these days they'd be regarded as politically incorrect. I'm not sure what that means, but here are some he remembered:

Q. Daddy, why can't I go outside and play with the other kids?

A. Shut up and deal.

Q. Mummy, why do I have to keep walking around in a circle?

A. Shut up or I'll nail your other foot to the floor.

Q. Mummy, Mummy can I lick the bowl?

A. No, just flush it like everybody else.

Q. Daddy, what's a vampire?

A. Shut up and drink your soup before it clots.

14. Pickpocket

Grandad said "I saw on the news tonight that a dwarf had gone to the races and was pickpocketed out of all his winnings.

How could anyone stoop so low?"

15. Cookies

"Grandma's joined Weightwatchers," Grandad announced yesterday. "But she needs you internet-savvy kids to help her. They've said she needs to disable her cookies."

16. Black Coffee

I was checking out Grandad's fridge, to make sure he was eating right, when I noticed an empty milk carton. I said "Do you want me to throw this out, Grandad?" He replied "No, of course not. I keep that in case one of my friends wants black coffee!" I'm still thinking about that.

17. Xmas Tree

Last Christmas, Grandad took us down to the nursery to get a real Christmas tree. We walked all around until we found the perfect sized one. The nursery offers an installation service, so the girl on the counter asked Grandad "Are you going to put it up yourself?"

Grandad said "Do I look like a pervert? No, we're putting it up in the living room."

The girl giggled and I asked Grandad what he meant.

He said "Ask your father."

18. Vacuum Cleaner

OMG. Grandad has always been a bit of a neat freak and he said to Grandma the other day "You should sell that vacuum cleaner. It's just gathering dust." She wasn't happy.

19. Dwarf

Which reminds me. I'm pretty sure this story isn't true, but last week Grandad told us that he was coming home from Centrelink when the car in front of him stopped suddenly and he rear ended it.

When the driver got out, he turned out to be a dwarf!

"I'm not happy," he said.

"So which one are you?" said Grandad.

I so hope this isn't true.

20. Magician

Honestly, now I'm older I realise I just walk into these.

Grandad tells me that when he was young he had a good friend who was a magician.

He specialised in sawing people in half. Had quite an act going.

And of course, Grandad tells me he had a big family and they were all friends.

So I ask what family did he have?

"Four half-sisters and two half-brothers" says Grandad, collapsing in laughter.

Lol.

21. Light Bulb

Grandad was telling us war stories. He had a close friend Peter who had lost an arm in Vietnam.

He was chatting with Peter who told him that he was about to change a light bulb.

Grandad said "Gosh that must be difficult with only one arm."

Peter said "Not really. I've still got the receipt."

22. Rounding Up

My Grandad had a farm. I asked him how many cows he had. "I counted them," he said "and it was 197. But when I rounded them up, it was 200." Grandad said it was a mathematical joke and I needed to think about it.

23. Grizzly

"A grizzly bear walks into a bar," said Grandad, "and the barman asks him what he wants to drink. The grizzly doesn't say a word, just looks at the barman. After a minute or so, he growls 'I'll have a beer, thanks.' 'Why the big pause?' asks the barman. 'I was born with them,' answers the grizzly."

24. Apple Tree

When we were driving somewhere, our Grandad would often ask us questions designed to improve our general knowledge. I don't think this one did though. "Do you know how many apples grow on an apple tree?" he asked. We admitted that we didn't. "All of them," we were told.

25. Velcro

"Never buy anything with Velcro," Grandad said suddenly, out of the blue. "Why not?" I asked. "It's a rip-off," said Grandad. I might have known!

26. Grandma

"I was at the bank with Grandma yesterday," said Grandad, "when she asked me to check her balance.

"So I pushed her over. Her balance was terrible.

"When we got home, Grandma asked me to pass her lipstick. But I accidentally passed her a glue stick instead. She's still not talking to me."

27. Rhyme

Grandad was taking me down to the playground when he said "Ask me what rhymes with orange."

Knowing this wasn't going to end well, but being curious about the answer, I dutifully asked "What rhymes with orange, Grandad?"

"No it doesn't," he replied.

Had to think about that one.

28. Unemployed

When my sister and I actually asked Grandad to tell us a joke (I know, what were we thinking?) he said "I know a lot of jokes about unemployed people, but none of them work."

29. Fancy-Dress

My Grandma's first name is Michelle. The other day, Grandad told us "You know, once upon a time, long before we got married, Grandma was my girlfriend. We went to a fancy-dress party at a friend's place, but we couldn't afford proper costumes. I went inside carrying Grandma on my back. My friend said 'mate, this is a fancy-dress party, what are you supposed to be?'

Grandad said "I've come as a turtle. This is Michelle."

Then Grandad told us he'd gone to another fancy-dress party disguised as a petrol bowser.

"I didn't fuel anyone," he admitted.

30. Dog Bike

"Do you know," said Grandad, getting that far away look in his eyes, "I once had a dog that would chase anyone on a bike? But I fixed the problem."

"What did you do, Grandad?" we asked.

"Easy peasy," said Grandad. "I took the mongrel's bike off him."

31. E.T.

My little brother watched E.T. on TV for the first time last night but was having trouble remembering 'extra-terrestrial' so he asked "Grandad, what's E.T. short for?"

"Probably because he's got really little legs," Grandad told him.

32. Millie

Grandma and Grandad have a family dog, Millie. Like Grandad, she's old but fit and has always been in our lives.

"I'm sorry, kids but I'm going to have to put Millie down."

"Oh no, Grandad," we cried. "What's wrong, is she sick?"

"No, she's just so damn heavy."

Grandad might have thought it was funny, but it took several ice creams before we forgave him.

33. French Fries

"Do you know where French Fries were first cooked?" asked Grandad.

"Umm... France?" I thought that seemed reasonable.

"No, Greece," said Grandad.

I didn't get it, until Grandad explained the difference and similarities between Greece and grease.

34. Factories

"So many factories try to produce products that are better than all their competitors."

Grandad was in business mode, or so we thought.

We waited on advice on how to make a success of our business.

"But the fact is," he continued, "most of them produce stuff that is, well, just ok.

"They're called satisfactories."

I don't think I'm going to be an entrepreneur. And that's Grandad's fault.

35. Ice Cream Van

A police car screamed by with its lights flashing and its sirens screaming.

"They won't sell much ice cream travelling at that speed," said Grandad.

36. Switzerland

We were totally surprised when Grandad told us "Grandma and I are thinking of moving to Switzerland."

"Why, Grandad?" we asked.

"Well," he said, "the flag is a big plus."

I had to Google it. Yes, Grandad, very funny.

37. Extension Cord

I reckon I got my own back on this one.

Grandad's got lots of tools and stuff.

I needed an extension cord, so I asked Grandad if I could borrow one of his.

"How long?" he asked. A perfectible reasonable question.

"All day, if you can afford it," I told him.

"You're getting old, kid," he said.

38. Genuine Joke

This is an actual, reasonably complicated joke my Grandad told, rather than just a quick comment.

I thought it was clever, but you have to be familiar with a particular song.

If you're not, ask your Mum.

Or watch the 1958 movie Inn of the Sixth Happiness. It's called *The Children's Marching Song*.

One day, a frog was swimming next to his lily-pad and decided that it could really use some improvements. Alas, the poor frog had no money to upgrade the lily-pad. One day, his friend said, "Hey... why don't you take out a loan?" The frog said, "Huh? Why would the bank give me a loan? I don't have anything of value!" His friend said, "Here... take this and use it for collateral." "Well, what is it?" the frog asked."

"It's just a simple knick-knack."

So the frog heads off to the bank, where he sees the loan officer, Ms. Patricia Black. The frog tells Ms. Black that he needs a loan, and she tells him that he needs some collateral. The frog offers the thing his friend gave him. Ms. Black looks at the thing and says, "I'm not sure what this is... let me get the bank manager." She gets the manager and asks him what the thing is.

"It's a knick-knack, Patty Black. Give the frog a loan!"

39. The Rash

I was having an allergic reaction to something I'd eaten at my grandparent's place and my face was breaking out in a bright pink rash.

"We'd better take her to ER," said Grandma.

But of course, Grandad said "Let's not make any rash decisions."

We high fived, but Grandma was really pissed.

40. Cold Fix

Winter was well and truly here and my grandson said to me "I'm so cold, Grandad."

I told him to go and stand in the corner.

"Why, Grandad?" he asked.

"Because it's 90 degrees there," I told him.

I'm trying to improve his understanding of geometry.

But he can be a bit obtuse.

His sister's very acute, though.

41. Cheesy

Grandad had been watching the news and said "It's a shame about that cheese factory that exploded in France.

"Apparently, there was nothing left but de Brie."

Later he muttered that they lost impact when you had to explain them.

42. Happy Returns

Grandad was looking puzzled, like he was having trouble remembering something.

"What's wrong, Grandad?" asked my sister.

"I can't remember any of my boomerang jokes," said Grandad.

"But I'm sure they'll come back to me."

43. It's About Time

We didn't want to be late for the movies, so I asked Grandad what the time was.

"It's hard to say," he said, looking at his watch. "It keeps changing."

44. Over Reaction

My little brother was crying because he'd stubbed his toe. Grandma was all over him, being comforting, but all Grandad could say was "Do you want me to call the toe truck?"

45. Not So Quiet

I'm sure Grandad told us this just because he knows we laugh at any story that has the word 'fart' in it. Mum just rolls her eyes.

"Grandma and I were at church last Sunday when she leans over and whispers in my ear 'I'm sorry, Bill, but I've just let go a silent fart. What should I do?"

"Getting a new battery for your hearing aid would be a good start," I told her.

Grandma doesn't wear a hearing aid, so I knew this wasn't true. We all giggled though.

46. Speed Bump

After Grandad slowed to a crawl to take the car over a speed bump, he said "I have an irrational fear of speed bumps."

We waited.

"But I'm slowly getting over it."

47. Camo Gear

I arrived at Grandad and Grandma's house wearing my new camo pants.

"Put some pants on immediately," said Grandad.

When I pointed out that I was wearing camouflage pants, Grandad said "Ah, that explains it."

He went on. "I've been searching for camouflage pants for years but haven't been able to find any."

I was about to tell him where they were in the store when I got the joke. Duh!

Unfortunately, Grandad wasn't finished.

"When I was doing National Service," he said "a group of us skived off to the movies instead of showing up for training.

"The sergeant hauled us up and demanded to know why we weren't at camouflage training.

"But we all were, Sarge," we said, "you just didn't see us."

48. Butter

"There's a rumour going around about butter," Grandad warned us.

"But don't spread it."

49. Spelling

I was so proud when I won first prize in the spelling bee that our local community hall ran as a fund-raiser.

Grandad said he was really proud of me. Said I was just like him.

"What do you mean, Grandad?" I asked.

"When I was your age," he said, "I was really good at spelling bees.

"It was the other words I had problems with."

50. Toilet Paper

I swear this is true.

Grandad says he makes them up on the spot, but I reckon he just has a store of them and trots out one to suit the situation.

We were in the supermarket and the lady in front of us dropped a roll of toilet paper.

It split open and started to roll down the aisle.

"Don't worry," said Grandad, "It's just trying to get to the bottom."

51. Grammar

"No one understands grammar any more," complained Grandad, "and I'm not talking about your grandmother here. Although that's probably true too. But I digress..."

"For example, you'd probably all say 'I run through the camp site,' wouldn't you?" he asked.

We admitted that sounded correct.

"Wrong," said Grandad, "it's 'I ran through the camp site.'

"Because it's past tents."

Mum said "Thank God you were never a teacher, Dad."

52. Glue

Although Grandad has a Kindle for all his plane flights, he's also a member of the local library and likes to talk about what he's reading.

So, during a lull in the conversation, I asked him "What are you reading at the moment, Grandad?"

His face brightened up. "Look, it sounds boring, but I'm reading the history of the development of super glue.

"I can't put it down."

53. The Farmer

The whole family was on a massive bike ride, from the summit of Mt Kosciusko in NSW to Marlow on the East coast of Victoria.

We rode over the Snowy mountains and passed several small townships and farms.

Grandad seemed really excited when we stopped at a small township for a coffee and snack.

"Did you see the award-winning farmer?" he asked.

"No, Grandad," we said (naively).

"He was out standing in his field."

Grandad, that was awful.

54. Colour Blind

Grandad had just come back from his biannual medical checkup and was looking shocked.

"What's wrong, Grandad?" I asked.

"It's awful," he sighed. "I've been diagnosed with colour-blindness."

I didn't know what to say. Until he said:

"It came completely out of the pink."

55. Titanic (again)

Us kids (Grandad days it's actually 'we kids') were really excited when we heard on the news that the place where the Titanic had sunk had been found and it was possible that they could raise it.

"Hmm..." said Grandad, "the difficulty is the way it's twitching."

"???"

"It's a nervous wreck."

56. The Bicycle

My brother was trying to use the kick-stand on his new bicycle to prop it up, but it kept falling over,

"There's a reason your bike won't stand up by itself," pontificated Grandad.

"It's two tyred."

57. Blueberries

"How do you tell the difference between elephants and blueberries?" asked Grandad.

"Blueberries are blue and elephants are grey," he answered himself, before we could say anything.

Unfortunately, there was more to come.

"What did Tarzan say when he saw the elephants coming?

"Here come the elephants.

"What did Jane say when she saw the elephants coming?

"Here come the blueberries.

"Jane was colour blind."

I told Grandad that was seriously awful.

58. Broken Arm

Having two older brothers, I've always been a bit of a tomboy and jumped at the chance to join one of my school's Rugby teams.

It was only my third game when I was tackled hard and came down on my left arm. The thought "that crack didn't sound good" was followed by searing pain.

It was an away game at a boarding school and they had a resident nurse. He gave me a shot of something wonderful that took most of the pain away.

The coach rang Mum, who was at an important meeting and she said, "I'll get her grandfather to take her to Emergency."

At the clinic, they X-Rayed my arm and told us to wait.

Half an hour later, the doctor came out and told Grandad "I'm afraid she's broken her arm in three places."

You can probably guess what Grandad said. "We'll be sure to keep her away from those three places in the future."

I laughed (the best medicine, I'm told) but the doc frowned disapprovingly.

59. Another Job

"Did you know," asked Grandad, "that I got canned from my job at the orange juice factory? Couldn't concentrate.

"But when they accepted me at the travel agency, I knew I was going places at last."

60. Fishy

Grandad explained puns to us long ago. He says they're a form of humour that both showcase and improve your grasp of the language.

So when he asked us to think of a fishy pun, we started to rack our brains.

Then he said "If you can't think of one, let minnow."

He followed this up by claiming he knew a fishy song and burst into "Salmon chanted evening..."

61. Shady

We'd been warned not to stand under trees in a storm, but it was lovely and sunny when Grandad said in a stern voice "Don't ever stand under those trees over there."

"Why not, Grandad?" we asked, "there's no lightning or anything."

"They just look pretty shady to me."

62. Jumper

We were on a long drive with Grandad, bored spitless (well, that's the polite version) and decided to play I spy.

When it was Grandad's turn, he said "I spy with my little eye... an animal that can jump higher than the Sydney Harbour Bridge."

We were all flummoxed. All we could see was an old cat, but even if we had seen a kangaroo, it still wouldn't have been right.

In the end, we gave up.

"It was the cat," said Grandad. "Actually, all animals can jump higher than the Sydney Harbour Bridge. Bridges can't jump at all."

Groans.

63. Stockholm

Mum and Dad had just finished explaining Stockholm syndrome to us.

"I once read a book about Stockholm syndrome," mused Grandad. "I hated it at first, but the longer I read it, the more I came to see how right it was and by the end I was loving it."

64. Escalators

We were in the department store when Grandad told us "Don't trust those escalators. They're up to something.

Groans.

"Except for that one over there. It's looking down."

65. Boomerang

My sister was practising in the park with the boomerang Auntie Ethel had given her for her birthday but was having no luck in persuading it to return.

"Do you know what they call a boomerang that won't come back?" asked Grandad.

"A stick."

Then he saw the tears in my sister's eyes, showed her how to throw the boomerang properly and bought both of us ice-creams.

I don't know how much longer she'll be able to get away with that little scam.

66. Hit Me

"I took the kids down to the park this morning, Liz" said Grandad to Mum.

"We were throwing the frisbee.

"I wondered why it was getting bigger and bigger.

"Then it hit me."

Mum rolled her eyes. "They're not getting any better, Dad."

Sometimes I forget that she's been listening to these her whole life. Gives new meaning to the term "long-suffering".

67. Password

"That online dating website I just joined said I needed a password of eight characters so I entered snow white and the seven dwarves.

"Then it said I needed some capital letters.

"I changed it to Snow White and the Seven Dwarves.

"Then it said spaces weren't allowed.

"So SnowWhiteandtheSevenDwarves.

"Then it said I had to include at least one number.

"My password became SnowWhiteandthe7Dwarves. Perfect, I thought.

"Sorry, that password is already taken."

"Grandad! Dating site??"

Grandad (trying to change the subject): "If I were Forrest Gump, my password would be 1Forrest1."

68. Comedian

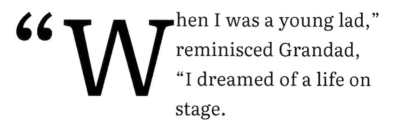"hen I was a young lad," reminisced Grandad, "I dreamed of a life on stage.

"I wanted to be a stand-up comedian.

"Everyone laughed when I told them of my ambition.

"Unfortunately, that was the last laugh I got."

69. Surprise

"I know it's hard for you kids to realise, but your Mum was young once too," said Grandad.

"She started using makeup when she was a bit older than you.

"I didn't mind. It's all part of growing up.

"But one day when she was fourteen, she plucked her eyebrows and then used eyebrow pencil to redraw them.

"When I told her that she'd drawn them much too high, she looked surprised."

I asked Mum about it. She said it was rubbish and that Grandad was just making another joke. Dunno, she looked a bit embarrassed though.

70. Terry-Dactyls

One of the things us kids really like about Grandad is that he doesn't mind jokes about farts, wees and poos. Actually, neither does Mum, but you can tell Dad gets a bit embarrassed.

Anyway, we were doing dinosaurs at school and Grandad had been really helpful with our project.

But he must of (sorry, have) got a bit bored, because he said "Crikey (he liked to channel Steve Irwin occasionally) can you imagine what it must have smelled like in the Jurassic period (which we had just been studying)?"

"Dinosaurs constantly farting, dinosaur poo everywhere and a constant stream of dinosaur wee."

We giggled, as was expected.

"Still," said Grandad, "at least you wouldn't have heard the pterodactyls going to the toilet."

"Umm... why not, Grandad?"

Grandad looked at us over the top of his glasses.

"Because the P is silent."

71. Missed

Grandad was watching the kettle boil.

"R.I.P." he said.

"What do you mean, Grandad?" I asked.

"The water," he said. "It'll be mist."

Seriously bad, but at least I learned that R.I.P. actually stands for the Latin "requiescat in pace" translated to the English "rest in peace". I mean, how many kids know that?

72. Relationship

Sometimes I think Grandad and Grandma's relationship is based entirely on humour and practical jokes.

Look, I'm old enough to know about sex and the fact that they had my Mum, my Auntie Ethel and three older brothers means that there was in fact a physical relationship involved.

Hard though that is to imagine.

And, to be perfectly frank, I have no wish to go there.

But, get this.

I was at their place last week and we're having breakfast.

"Gosh, Michelle," says Grandad, "have you noticed how muggy it is outside?"

Then he brings out a breakfast bowl of coffee and starts sipping it.

"I swear, Bill," says Grandma, "if all our coffee mugs are on the lawn, I'm leaving you."

They were, of course and she didn't, of course.

73. Bouncy Bouncy

"I thought this was such a good idea," said Grandad.

"What?" I asked, expecting the worst.

"Replacing our old bed with a trampoline," he said.

"Oh no," I replied. "What did Grandma say?"

"She hit the roof."

Why am I not surprised?

74. iStuff Sync

Grandad's an iStuff fan. He has an iPhone, two iPod Classics (he says why would you have an iPod Touch it's just a retarded iPhone) and an iPad.

So when he asked us what happens when you drop your iPhone and iPad in the swimming pool, we really thought he was serious. Especially when he says Android demonstrates everything that's meant by "too many cooks spoil the broth". Sorry, I digress.

"They sync," he said.

Only a person who spent their career in IT would sink, sorry think, that was funny.

75. SPAM

Did you know that spam is actually a brand of cooked meat made popular during and after World War 2? It's sold in 41 countries on six continents and trademarked in over 100 countries. In 2012, the eight billionth can of Spam was sold.

But because it was regarded as "fake ham" its name was given to fake emails, or more generally to any sort of unwanted or unsolicited email.

After Grandad explained all that (yawn) we understood what he meant.

"I was worried about an email I received telling me that processed meat can cause cancer," said Grandad.

"But then I realised that it was probably spam."

76. Police Dogs

"That's just shocking," said Grandad.

"Some bold as brass thieves have been breaking into the police compound and stealing the puppies in training to be police dogs.

"Fortunately, the police have several leads."

77. Six-Pack

Grandad was standing in front of the mirror, admiring his six pack, when Grandma walked in.

"Put them back in the fridge, Bill" she said.

"The kids are coming over later, and they'll want a cold beer."

78. Doctor, Doctor

"Hey, who wants to hear a Doctor, Doctor joke?" asked Grandad.

We had about 1,000 km ahead of us, so anything was good at this stage.

"Go for it, Grandad" we enthused.

Oh, the wisdom of hindsight.

"Doctor, doctor, I think I have five legs."

"How do your pants fit?"

"Like a glove."

"Doctor, doctor, I've got a strawberry up my bum."

"I've got some cream for that."

"Doctor, doctor, I'm so worried about the Australian cricket team."

"Howzat?"

"Doctor, doctor, I keep hearing 'The green, green grass of home' in my head."

"Sounds like Tom Jones syndrome."

"Is that common?"

"It's not unusual..."

79. Hamster

I really love my granddaughter and when her pet hamster escaped from its cage, I spent four hours looking for it.

No luck though.

It wasn't in the pub.

80. No Charge

I introduced Grandad to Gumtree yesterday.

He was so excited.

Gave away all his old batteries.

Free of charge.

81. Golf

Dad and Grandad were talking golf, as they often did. Mum says they're golf tragics.

"Did I tell you about this new golf ball I've got, Mike?" asked Grandad.

"No, what about it?"

"It's brilliant. You can't lose it. It glows in the dark, floats on water and automatically drifts to shore and, best of all, emits a radio beacon that I can home in on with an app on my phone."

(Grandad is the most tech-savvy old person I know. He once told me he finds pressing F5 refreshing).

"That's fantastic," said Dad, "must have cost heaps."

"Not at all. I found it."

82. Lifts

"I don't know why," said Grandad, "but recently Grandma has become terrified of lifts.

"But don't worry, we're taking steps to avoid them."

83. Big Numbers

My little brother has a fascination with numbers, especially big ones and is always asking Grandad what's the next big number after a million, a billion and so on.

So Grandad says to him "How many South Americans does it take to screw in a lightbulb?

"A Brazillion," he answers his own question.

The littlie loves numbers but geography isn't his strong suit, so out came the globe of the world.

Then Grandad had one for me. I'm going to a private girls' school next year. It has a bit of a reputation for entitlement. Undeserved, I hope, or at least applicable only to a minority.

"How many (school name withheld) girls does it take to screw in a lightbulb?"

"A Brazilian?" I guessed.

"Just one," said Grandad. "She holds it still while the rest of the world revolves around her."

84. Binge Watching

"Last night," Grandad told us, "Grandma and I watched three DVDs back to back."

Before we could ask what they were, he went on to say "Unfortunately for me, Grandma insisted on being the one facing the television."

85. Twitter

I told you Grandad was pretty tech savvy, so we weren't surprised when he told us that Grandma was pretty upset about his obsession with Twitter.

"What did you do, Grandad?" we asked.

"I told her that was totally #unfair, but that I would try to make a #new-year-resolution to #quitnow.

"Showed her I was serious by tweeting it to all my followers."

86. Waitress

"When your Mum was a teenager," Grandad told us, "she was really excited at being offered a job as a waitress at a local restaurant.

"She told them she couldn't wait.

"They said that was too bad, but they were sure they could find someone who could."

87. EpiPen

"I'll always treasure this EpiPen," said Grandad. "My best friend gave it to me as he was dying.

"It seemed really important to him that I have it.

"He pressed it into my hand and said 'Bill take this and use it, please. I can't.' How selfless was that?"

Mum said "Dad, don't tell the kids jokes like that."

We didn't get it anyway.

But Grandad kept going.

"While I was at the funeral parlour, a man tried to sell me a coffin.

"I told him it was the last thing I need."

88. So Cross

Grandad has what seems like an infinite store of "What do you get when you cross (something) with (another thing) jokes." Here are some of them:

What do get when you cross a Labrador Retriever with a Tortoise?
An animal that goes to the newsagent and fetches last week's newspaper.

What do get when you cross a hen with gunpowder?
An eggsplosion.

What do get when you cross a chicken with a dog?
Pooched eggs.

What do get when you cross a policeman and an artist?
A brush with the law.

What do get when you cross a chicken and a skunk?

A fowl smell.

What do get if you cross the Atlantic with the Titanic?

About half way.

89. Holy

I heard Dad say to Mum "Look Liz, I've got a hole in my sock."

And then Grandad chipped in "Me too. That's how I get my foot into it."

90. Happy

"You know," mused Grandad, "your Grandma and I were deliriously happy for twenty years."

"What happened then?" we asked.

"Then we met."

"But all jokes aside, our wedding was a beautiful affair. Even the wedding cake was in tiers."

91. Flamingo

"Do you know why a Flamingo stands on one leg?" Grandad asked us, standing on one leg by way of illustration.

We shook our heads.

"Well if it didn't, it would fall over," he said.

Unfortunately, he went on.

"Grandma told me I had to stop impersonating a flamingo.

"But I showed her. I put my foot down."

92. No Coffin

"I had a friend who'd made a lot of money by inventing a really effective treatment for sore throats," Grandad told us.

"When he died, his family invited all of his customers to the funeral.

"There was no coffin."

93. Philosopher

Grandad does sometimes get philosophical so we weren't too surprised when he looked deeply thoughtful and almost whispered "I was lying in bed last night, gazing up at the stars and thinking..."

There he paused, seeming reluctant to go on.

I broke the silence.

"What were you thinking, Grandad?"

"Where the hell is my roof?"

94. The Telephone

"Someone was telling me," said Grandad, "that they thought one of the most useful inventions was the first telephone.

"What do you kids think?"

As I'm due to get my first very own mobile phone next birthday, I definitely agreed.

"No," said Grandad, "the first telephone was totally useless.

"The second one was much more useful."

95. Glue Cake

Yesterday, Grandad showed us how to make a kite that flew much better than "that cheap plastic rubbish" you buy in the shops.

It was covered in coloured paper from Officeworks and Grandad showed us how to make paste from flour and water to stick the paper around the string.

Today, he was discussing cooking with Mum.

"There's something I don't understand about cooking, Liz."

"There's plenty you don't understand about cooking, Dad" said Mum, who'd sometimes entertain us with stories of Grandad's cooking disasters when Grandma was away or sick. "But what in particular?"

"Well," said Grandad, "if you mix flour and water, you get glue.

"If you add egg, you get cake.

"What happens to the glue?"

96. Paddling

We had a great time on the river yesterday.

Mum and my big brother were in one canoe and Grandad and I were in another.

It was lovely and peaceful, except for two women in a canoe ahead of us, who never stopped talking.

"You know what they are?" said Grandad, fairly loudly.

"Kayakkers."

97. Good Prognosis

Grandma had just come back from hospital after a minor operation. We asked Grandad how she was.

"Unfortunately, the doctors had to remove everything on her left side."

We looked at Grandad in horror.

"She's all right now."

98. Priorities

Grandad had a ticket to the Grand Final but realised it clashed with his and Grandma's 50th anniversary dinner celebration.

He rang his best mate Len to see if he wanted to go instead.

"You'd be picking up Michelle and taking her to the restaurant around 7 o'clock," he told him. "There'll be plenty of other family there."

99. Left Luggage

"When Grandma and I were travelling in Europe," Grandad informed us, "the airline misplaced all our luggage. They never recompensed us and said it was our fault for not having insurance.

"I was so mad, I took them to court."

"What happened, Grandad?"

"I lost my case."

100. The Bard

My brother was studying Shakespeare in English Lit. class at school.

Grandad is quite knowledgeable about Shakespeare's plays and we were discussing some stuff with him when he said "The one thing they never tell you is why Shakespeare's wife left him."

"Why did she, Grandad?" asked my brother. Naively, I thought.

"Too many dramas," answered Grandad.

I bet my brother tells the teacher that tomorrow.

101. Speechless

Grandad was looking really angry, so we asked him what was wrong.

"I bought a brand-new Thesaurus today.

"When I got home and opened it, I found all the pages were blank!

"I'm so angry but have no words to describe it."

102. Swifties

Here's a bonus for you.

Quick one-liners that will seal your reputation as a smart-arse if you can produce them at just the right time.

1. Two peanuts were walking down the street. One was a salted.
2. When you ask your Dad if he's alright, he'll probably answer "no, I'm half left."
3. 5/4 of people admit they're bad with fractions.
4. "How do I look?" "With your eyes, like everyone else."
5. I hate camping. Everything's so in tents.
6. I'm only familiar with 25 letters in the alphabet. I don't know why.
7. What did the buffalo say to his son when he dropped him off at school? Bison.

8. What do you call someone with no body and no nose? Nobody knows.

9. Why did the crab never share? Because he's shellfish.

10. Whiteboards are remarkable, aren't they?

11. Twins that move in together are going back to being womb mates.

12. I used to be a banker, but I lost interest.

13. The coffee filed a police report after it got mugged.

14. I'd like to open a restaurant on the Moon, but it wouldn't have any atmosphere.

15. The shovel was a ground-breaking invention.

16. I used to hate facial hair. But then it grew on me.

17. Jokes about German sausage are the wurst.

18. A fish with no eyes is called... a fsh.

19. Two men were convicted of stealing a calendar and got six months each.
20. I dreamt I was a muffler and woke up exhausted.
21. I'm dreading Jamaican hairstyle day at work tomorrow.
22. Don't drink coffee. It's for mugs.
23. Edam cheese is made backwards.
24. French people eat snails because they don't like fast food.
25. When a book falls on your head, you've only got yourshelf to blame.

If you've enjoyed this book (actually, even if you haven't) why not head over to phil-lancaster.com/101-jokes-audio and get the free audio version, read by the author?

Play it in the car and enjoy the groans from your passengers.

Printed in Poland
by Amazon Fulfillment
Poland Sp. z o.o., Wrocław

51423956R00075